Maui and his Brothers

Adapted by Sheila Lane and Marion Kemp

Illustrations by Jenny Mumford

Take Part Starters

Level 3

Ward Lock Educational Co. Ltd.

Ward Lock Educational Co. Ltd.
T.R. House
Christopher Road
East Grinstead
RH19 3BT

A member of the Ling Kee Group
London · Hong Kong · New York · Singapore

This adaptation published 1989

ISBN 0 7062 5142 3

Printed in Hong Kong.

Contents

★ This sign means that you can make the sounds which go with the story.

This story is from New Zealand. It is about a boy called Maui (say 'mar-we') who was thrown into the sea when he was a baby.

Maui lay on a bed of seaweed. Jellyfish wrapped themselves round his tiny body and kept him warm. Fish brought him food.

Years later, Maui came back from the sea. His brothers were *not* pleased to see him.

Maui Finds his Brothers

This is Ra, the eldest of the brothers.
Ra's name means SUN.

Rangi is Maui's second brother.
Rangi's name means SKY.

Kiwi is the youngest until Maui comes back. Kiwi's name means BIRD.

Maui's brothers are sitting outside their sleeping hut.
Maui is standing in front of them holding his sleeping mat.

Ra Go away! Take your sleeping mat and go away from here.

Rangi We don't want you here.

Kiwi Go back to the sea.

Maui But I'm your brother.

Ra Can't you see that we don't want you?

Rangi Go back to where you came from.

Kiwi Go back to the sea.

Maui But why? What's wrong with me?

Kiwi We don't like the look of you.

Rangi And we don't like the smell of you.

Kiwi You smell of the sea.

Rangi And seaweed and jellyfish.

Ra Anyway, you don't know your place in the family. I'm Number One around here.

Rangi And I'm Number Two.

Kiwi I'm Number Three.

Maui Which means that I can be Number Four. What's wrong with that?

Ra Well . . . nothing . . . IF we let you stay.

Rangi Yes . . . IF we let you stay.

Kiwi IF we do!

Ra If we let you stay, you'll have to remember that I'm Ra, The Great, who is named after the sun in the sky.

Rangi And I'm Rangi. I'm named after the sky itself.

Kiwi And I'm Kiwi.
I'm named after the great bird.

Maui Well . . . I'm Maui — the one who has come home to live with his brothers.

Ra If you want us to keep you, Maui, you'll have to show us what you can do.

Maui What do you want me to do?

Kiwi SING!
Can you sing like a bird?
Go on, Maui, sing!

Rangi Yes, sing to us, Maui.

Maui All right! Listen!
★ Tr-coo! ★ Tr-coo!

Ra So! You *can* sing, Maui! But can you FLY?
Can you fly like a bird.

Rangi Let's see you fly!

Kiwi IF YOU CAN!

Maui All right! Watch me fly! ★ Up I go! ★ Tr-coo!
Look at me! Up! Up!

Rangi Look at him! Look at him!

Kiwi Look! He CAN fly!

Ra This brother of ours has *magic* powers.
Now . . . shall we keep him, or shall we send him away?

Rangi I say, keep him. What do you say, Kiwi?

Kiwi Well . . . yes . . .
Let's keep him.

Maui Tr-coo! ★ Tr-coo! ★ I'm back!
You've seen what I can do, brothers.
So . . . WILL YOU LET ME STAY?

Ra If we let you stay, Maui, you'll have to do as you're told.

Maui I will! I will! Just keep me! Keep me and I'll be a good brother to you all.

Ra You'll have to remember that I'm Number One around here.

Maui I will! I promise!

Rangi And I come next after Ra. I'm Number Two.

Kiwi And then me!
I'm Number Three.

Maui Yes! Yes! And I'll be Number Four.

Ra All right! We'll keep you — and we'll see how we all get on together.

Maui Plays with Fire

Maui and his brothers are blowing on their earth-oven. ★

Maui I'm hungry!

Rangi We're all hungry, brother.

Maui I want my breakfast.

Kiwi We all want our breakfast, brother.

Rangi We can't cook our breakfast if we have no fire.

Ra We must blow harder on the ashes of our earth-oven then our fire will come to life. ★

Maui But it's not coming to life. Look at it!

Ra It will come in time. Now . . . let's all blow together. ★

Rangi No, Maui! Don't blow like that!

Maui Look at me! I'm covered in ashes and we still have no fire.

Kiwi You must blow like this. ★

Maui This is no way to live. We should have our *own* fire power.

Ra The great fire goddess keeps all the fire power for herself.

Maui Why should she have it all? Let's go and get some. Where does she live?

Ra She lives on the other side of the mountain. They say it is a terrible place.

Maui I'll go and get some. I'm not afraid.

Rangi You can't do that, brother. No one can get near her.

Kiwi It is too hot.

Maui I don't care how hot it is. I'll fly over the mountain and get some fire power. I'm not afraid. ★

Kiwi Look at him! Look at him!

Rangi I wish I could fly like that.

Ra How handsome he looks as he flies in the air.

Rangi And he knows it too!

Ra But will he be able to bring us fire power for our earth-oven?

Kiwi No!

Rangi He will never be able to do that.

Ra All we can do now is to sit here and wait.
But . . . I wonder . . .

Kiwi What is it, Ra?

Ra I wonder if our Number Four brother will ever come back.

Rangi Let's watch the sky.

Kiwi The sky! Look at it!

Rangi Why is the sky so red this morning?

Kiwi Brothers! Brothers!
How hot it is!

Ra Could it be that our brother has reached the place where the fire goddess lives?

Rangi Could it be that Maui and the fire goddess are AT WAR?

Kiwi Brothers! LOOK!

Rangi The grass! It's drying up in the heat.
Everything is drying up.

Ra Look over on the mountain! The trees are on fire!
★ Listen! Do you hear that crackling sound? ★

Kiwi Look! Look!
Look up, in the sky!

Rangi Where?

Kiwi Over there!
It looks like a bird.

Rangi No! It's not a bird! It's Maui! It's our brother!

Ra Something is wrong. See how slowly he flies.

Rangi Fly this way, Maui!

Kiwi Maui! MAUI!

Ra Look at this body. He's burned all over by the flames.

Rangi Over here, Maui! Come and rest.

Kiwi Sit down and rest, brother.

Rangi Did you make war with the fire goddess?

Kiwi And did the fire goddess burn you, brother?

Ra I want to know if you got the fire power, so that we can keep our earth-oven alight all night.

Rangi Yes, the fire! Where is it?

Kiwi Give it to us, brother.

Ra He hasn't got it! I do believe he hasn't got the fire power after all.

Maui So you want fire power, brothers.

Ra Don't play tricks with us, Maui. Have you got fire power or haven't you?

Maui Oh, yes! I've got fire power.

Kiwi Then, where is it?

Rangi Give it to us — if you've got it.

Maui It's THERE . . . and THERE . . . and THERE!

Ra What does he mean? He's pointing at those gum trees.

Rangi He's playing tricks on us.

Maui No, I'm not! Fire power is in those trees. It has been there for millions of years.

Rangi Trees are made of wood . . .

Kiwi . . . and wood will burn.

Ra So if a tree had fire power it would burn up. You're stupid, Maui!

Rangi Yes, stupid!

Kiwi STUPID!

Maui You're the stupid ones, brothers. The fire seed is in the trees. It has always been there.

Kiwi How can FIRE BE IN A TREE?

Maui Look, I'll show you. All you have to do is to take two sticks from a tree . . . like this. ★

Rangi But how do you MAKE FIRE?

Maui Watch me! ★ Rub the two sticks together, like this. ★

Kiwi There is no fire.

Rangi There is nothing.

Ra You are tricking us, Maui.

Kiwi NO! He isn't!
Look! LOOK!

Maui The fire seed is beginning to come. ★ WATCH!

Kiwi Look! LOOK!
It's coming!
The fire is coming! ★

Rangi Look, Ra! Maui has made fire from the fire seed in the sticks.

Ra Do you mean that it was always there, but we didn't know how to get it?

Maui Yes, that's right. And I nearly got burned to death going to see that terrible fire goddess.

Rangi But how did you find out that the old fire goddess kept the fire seed in the wood of trees?

Maui Well . . . as I was flying in the air, I saw her rubbing sticks together.

Kiwi Did she see you, Maui?

Maui Yes, she did. And as soon as she saw me, she blew on the fire she'd made so that the flames licked up into the sky.

Rangi So that was how you got your burns.

Kiwi And that was why the sky was so red.

Ra Was the old fire goddess very angry, Maui?

Maui Yes, she was! She blew the flames until they reached my poor body. Look at it!

Ra So now you have an enemy, brother. The fire goddess will never forgive you for stealing her secret.

Rangi Yes, she has lost her fire power now.

Kiwi She will NEVER forgive you, Maui.

Maui I don't care! I don't care about her. I don't care about ANYBODY!

Maui's Tricks

Maui's brothers are sitting outside the sleeping-hut cooking fish in their earth-oven. ★

Rangi There! We can make a fire and cook our fish whenever we like now — thanks to Maui.

Kiwi Where is Maui? Where is he?

Rangi I saw him flying away over the trees.

Ra I wish he would fly away and never come back.

Kiwi How can you say that, Ra?

Rangi Maui has given us the secret of fire power.

Ra You do nothing but talk about Maui! Have you forgotten who is Number One around here?

Kiwi No.

Rangi We know that you are our Number One brother.

Ra Maui has forgotten! He has forgotten that I am Ra.
I am Ra, who is named after the great sun in the sky.

Rangi Look! Here he comes! Here comes
our Number Four brother. ★

Kiwi How I wish I could fly in the sky like Maui.

Maui I heard what you said, Kiwi.
But you can't fly like me
and you never will fly.

Kiwi How do you know that?

Maui I just know! Anyway, you are named
after the Kiwi bird and Kiwis can't fly.

Ra You think too much of yourself, Maui. Have you
forgotten the promise you made when we
took you in?

Maui Promise? What did I promise?

Rangi You said, 'Keep me and I will be a good brother
to you all.'

Maui But I AM a good brother to you all. Didn't I bring you the secret of fire power. Have you forgotten that?

Ra No, we haven't forgotten, Maui. But we're getting tired of your talk and we're getting tired of your tricks.

Maui Tricks! What are you talking about?

Ra I saw you down by the river yesterday.

Maui What of it? I *can* go down to the river, I suppose.

Ra You were teasing the birds.

Kiwi What did he do, Ra?

Ra He was holding their heads under the water.

Rangi Maui! That's a bad thing to do.

Kiwi Why did you do it, Maui?

Maui Because the birds wouldn't obey me. I was thirsty, so I told them to fetch me some water from the river.

Kiwi Did they fetch you some water?

Maui No, they didn't! So I punished them.

Ra Someone will punish you one day, Maui.

Maui You're jealous of me, Ra. You're jealous because I have magic powers. But don't worry brothers! I only punish those who don't obey me.

Kiwi What do you mean?

Maui I mean that I reward those who *do* obey me.

Rangi Listen to him! Magic powers!

Maui Today I rewarded the crow. It fetched me some water in its ears, so I rewarded it.

Kiwi What did you do?

Maui I pulled its legs to make them longer!

Ra WHO DO YOU THINK YOU ARE? MAUI?

Maui Listen brothers! Listen to my words!
I am Maui-the-bold,
I am Maui-the-strong,
I am Maui-the-powerful,
I sing a magic song.

Rangi Listen to his talk!

Ra You are Maui-the-one-who-thinks-too-much-of-himself!

Maui You're all jealous of me, but I don't care. I shan't change. I shall be the same FOR EVER!

Ra Then we don't want you with us, Maui. We don't want a brother who thinks too much of himself.

Kiwi No, we don't want you, Maui.

Rangi Come on, brothers. Let's leave him and go fishing.

Maui Fishing! I'd like to go fishing. Take me with you, brothers, and I will bring you luck with my magic powers.

Ra NO! We don't want you.

Maui You don't like me, Ra. You don't like me because my magic powers make me greater than you.

Ra I don't like you because you are unkind, Maui. Yesterday I saw you put a barb on your fish hook.

Rangi If you did that, the fish had no chance to get away.

Kiwi That was a bad thing to do, Maui.

Maui BAD! How stupid you all are. Why do you go fishing if you want some of the fish to get away?

Ra We need fish to eat, but we must all fish fairly, brother.

Maui Listen, brothers! I can catch a fish so big that you won't be able to eat it all before it goes bad.

Kiwi No! We don't want you with us Maui.

Rangi For the last time — GO AWAY!

Maui All right, I'll go!
But you'll be sorry.

Maui Fishes up Land

The three brothers are paddling their canoe out to sea. ★

Rangi It's good to be out at sea, brothers.

Kiwi And no Maui!

Ra That brother of ours doesn't know his place.

Kiwi His head is too big!

Rangi And he plays unkind tricks.

Ra We're better off without him. Come on, brothers! Let's paddle hard! ★

Kiwi Brothers! Look over there!

Rangi Where?

Kiwi Up there — in the sky.

Rangi It looks like some kind of bird.

Kiwi No! It's not a bird, brothers.
It's MAUI!

Rangi So our brother has come after us.

Ra Yes! He waited for us to paddle out to sea and then flew from the shore.

Rangi What do you want, Maui?

Maui I want to go fishing with you.

Kiwi NO! GO AWAY!

Maui I'm here! I'm standing on your canoe, you can't get rid of me.

Rangi Oh, yes we can!

Ra You're not coming with us, Maui. Brothers! Turn the canoe round and paddle back to the shore.

Maui You can't get rid of me, brothers.

Ra Rangi! Kiwi! Throw him into the sea!

Maui I don't care if you do. You can't drown me! I shall just climb out of the water and follow you back to the shore.

Kiwi What can we do, Ra?

Rangi How can we get rid of him?

Maui You can't get rid of me because I've got magic power.
Listen brothers! Listen and watch!
'O great blue sea
Stretch out for me!'

Ra What's happening? ★ The canoe is rocking from side to side. ★

Kiwi It's taking us out to sea.

Maui That's where I want to go. That's where the best fish are.

Kiwi How do you know where the best fish are?

Maui I am Maui-the-wise.
The sea tells me its secrets.

Rangi The sea is too deep for our fishing lines out here.

Maui You're wrong, brother. We shall have good fishing in the deep water. You'll see!

Ra You'd better be right, Maui, or you may find that the fish use you for bait!

Maui Don't you understand, Ra?
I am Maui-the-bold,
I am Maui-the-strong,
I am Maui-the-powerful . . .
Brothers! We have reached the place!

Ra Place! What place! We've never been here before. None of us know this place.

Maui But I know! Your Number Four brother knows all things.

Ra You'd better be right about this, brother.

Maui We're there! We've reached the place — I know it! Throw down the anchor, brothers!

Ra Anchor! This water is too deep for our anchor.

Maui Do as I say! Throw down the anchor — NOW!

Kiwi Let's do what he says, Ra. ★

Maui Let down your fishing lines!

Rangi Help me to hold them, Kiwi. ★
Now . . .OVER THEY GO! ★

Kiwi Down . . . down . . . down!

Rangi They're down as far as they will go, Maui.

Maui Now . . . we must wait. Soon you will all know why
I've brought you here, out to the deep water.

Rangi I think . . . I think . . . I think . . .
Yes! I've got one! ★

Kiwi And look at this! ★

Ra So our Number Four brother really knows where the big fish live.

Maui What did I tell you, brothers?

Ra You told us that you could help us to catch a fish so big that we couldn't eat it all before it went bad.

Kiwi And he has! He has!

Rangi We have never caught so many big fish before.
Look! More . . . and more! ★

Kiwi Maui has magic power over the fish.
Look Ra! Our boat is full.

Ra Stop fishing, brothers! This boat of ours is too full already.

Rangi It's very low in the water.

Kiwi It's much too low, Ra!
Look! We shall soon sink!

Maui Don't worry, brothers! We haven't finished yet.

Ra We HAVE finished, I say.

Maui NO! Not yet.

Ra We shall sink if we take in any more fish. Paddle back to the shore, brothers — before it's too late.

Maui NO! Not yet! I want my turn.

Kiwi But you have no hook.

Maui I have! Look at this.

Rangi Where did you get that hook from?

Maui I made it and it has magic power.
So . . . it's my turn now.

Ra No, Maui! The canoe is full.
Paddle back to the shore, brothers.

Maui NO, I say! Give me my turn — or I'll sink the canoe.

Kiwi Let him have his turn, Ra!

Ra Very well — but this brother of ours makes trouble wherever he goes.

Rangi Maui's hook is going down fast. Look!

Kiwi MAUI! MAUI!

Maui What is it? What's the matter?

Rangi The canoe is taking in water! ★
We're sinking!

Ra We must bail out the water!
KIWI! RANGI! Help me to bail the water
out of the canoe. ★

Maui Stop, brothers! Stop your noise!

Ra We MUST bail out, Maui, or the canoe will sink.

Maui Listen brothers! Listen to my words:
Blow wind of the north,
Blow wind of the south,
And take these words
From my open mouth.

Ra What are you doing, Maui? Your hook must be at the bottom of the sea.

Kiwi WE shall soon be at the bottom of the sea!

Rangi But look at him brothers! How strong he is!

Ra Maui! Maui! You are pulling too hard.

Rangi You'll have us all in the sea.

Kiwi Let the line go!

Ra LET IT GO, MAUI!

Maui LET GO! I won't let go! I'll never . . . never . . . NEVER LET GO!

Ra Bail out the water, brothers! Bail out!
Bail out, or we shall sink! ★

Maui Listen, brothers! Listen to my words!
My line is straight,
My line is strong,
My hook stays fast
As I sing my song.

All 3 Brothers Let go, Maui! LET GO!

Kiwi Look at him! He's mad!

Rangi We shall all drown!

Ra The waters of the sea
are bubbling and boiling. ★
For the last time —
MAUI, LET GO!

Maui Listen brothers! Listen to my words!
O land of the sea
Come now to me.
Come up to my hand
O great new land.

Rangi LOOK!

Kiwi LOOK, BROTHERS!

Ra Maui has fished up LAND!

All 3 Brothers LAND! LAND!

Maui Remember what I told you, brothers:
I am Maui-the-bold,
I am Maui-the-strong,
I am Maui-the-powerful,
I sing a magic song.

Ra Maui . . . the bold . . .

Rangi Maui . . . the strong . . .

Kiwi Maui . . . our brother . . .

All 3 Brothers MAUI . . . LIVE LONG!

Fast Tracks

Tracking Through Myths and Legends

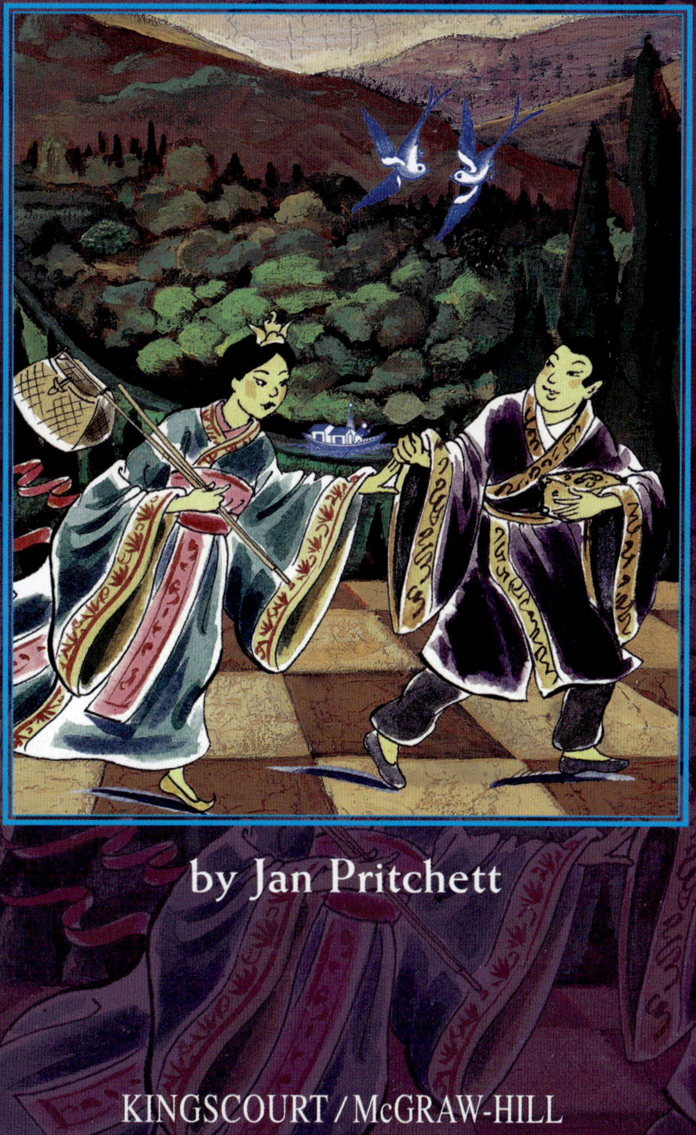

by Jan Pritchett

KINGSCOURT / McGRAW-HILL

Tracking Through Myths and Legends

Rigby is part of Harcourt Education, a division of
Reed International Books Australia Pty Ltd ABN 70 001 002 357.

Text by Jan Pritchett
Edited by Celia Purdey
Designed by Jennifer Johnston
Illustrated by Betty Greenhatch, pp. 26–31; Tracie Grimwood, pp. 8–15, 18, 20, 22–23; Sonia Kretschmar, cover, pp. 6, 24

Published in the United Kingdom by Kingscourt/McGraw-Hill, a division of the MH Companies. Originally published in Australia by Rigby Heinemann, a division of Reed International Books Australia Pty Ltd.

Acknowledgments
for photographs: Malcolm Cross, pp. 24, 27, 34—39.
for text: David Higham Associates for the story "The Willow Pattern" from *Realms of Gold: Myths and Legends From Around the World* by Ann Pilling. © Ann Pilling 1993.

KINGSCOURT/McGRAW-HILL
Shoppenhangers Road, Maidenhead
Berkshire, SL6 2QL
Telephone: 01628 502730
Fax: 01628 635895

www.kingscourt.co.uk
E-mail: enquiries@kingscourt.co.uk

Printed in Australia by Advance Press

10 9 8 7 6 5 4 3 2 1

ISBN: 0-07-710339-4

Contents

Introduction to Myths and Legends

Myths and legends are traditional stories, originally told by storytellers. Every culture in the world has its own traditional stories.

Myths are stories explaining the wonders around us. They tell about the things in the world that never change. Myths tell about the origin of the world and the arrival of humans. There are also explanatory myths that explain how and why natural events, such as the changing seasons or thunder and lightning, occur.

Over the centuries, myths and real events have merged, becoming tales of dangerous adventures, battles with monsters and giants, and of rescuing victims in distress. However, one feature is always the same in myths—good triumphs over evil.

Legends are stories of famous heroes and heroines who lived in a specific time. No one knows if the heroes and heroines are purely imaginary characters or based on real people such as Robin Hood and his band of thieves. Occasionally, the hero or heroine of a legend has great powers. He or she is also brave, good and honest, and faces a villain who tries to trick him or her.

Mercury
Pegasus
Medusa
Venus
Bacchus

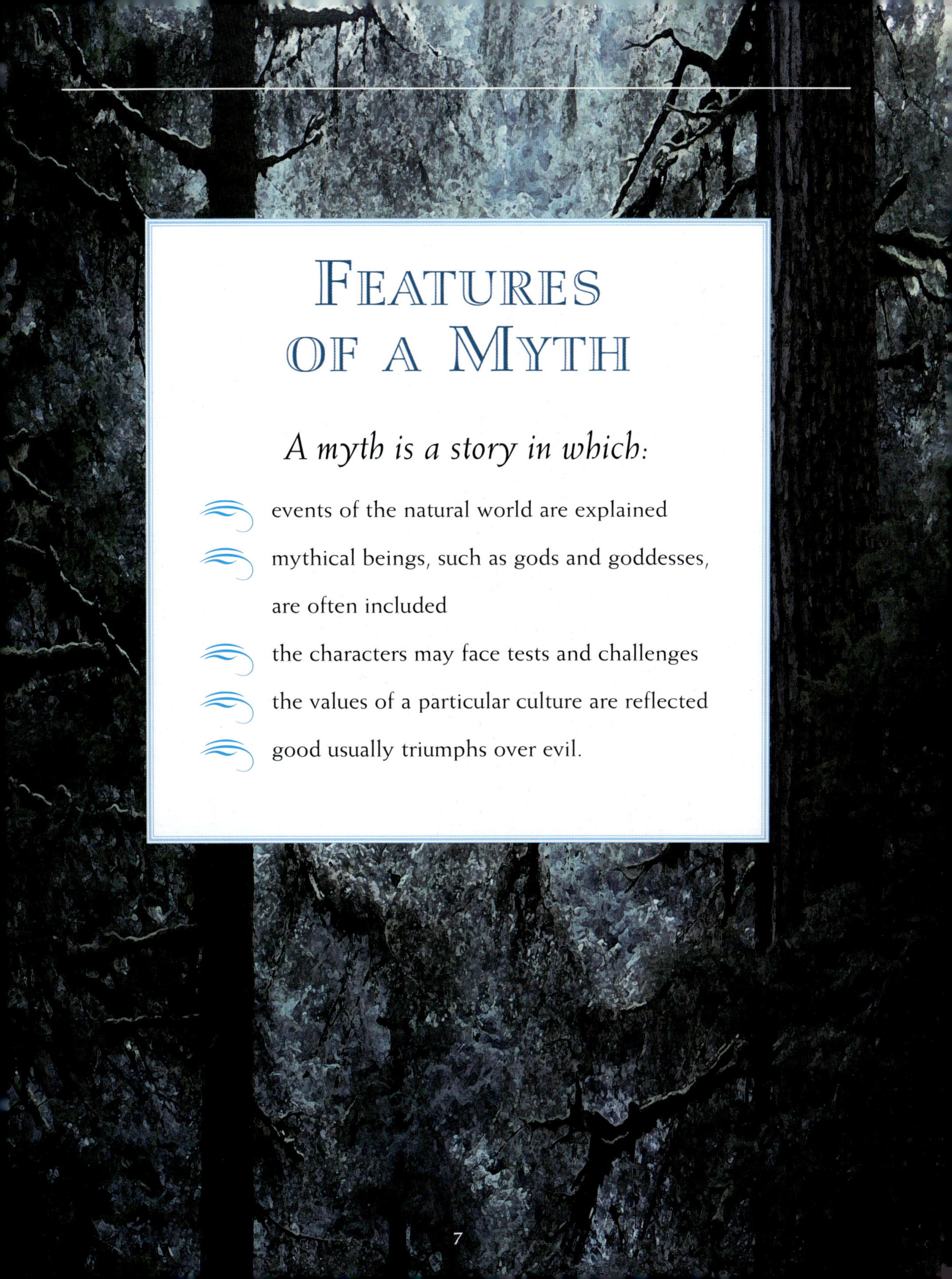

Features of a Myth

A myth is a story in which:

- events of the natural world are explained
- mythical beings, such as gods and goddesses, are often included
- the characters may face tests and challenges
- the values of a particular culture are reflected
- good usually triumphs over evil.

PERSEPHONE

The story of Persephone is a Greek myth.

The Ancient Greeks believed that at the beginning of time, gods defeated the giants that ruled the world. The gods and goddesses lived at Mount Olympus. The god **Zeus** *was the ruler of the gods and ruled the sky, his brother* **Poseidon** *ruled the sea, and another brother* **Hades** *ruled the Underworld. There were gods and goddesses to control all the events on Earth.* **Demeter** *was the goddess of agriculture and growing things,* **Helios** *was the sun god, and* **Hermes** *was the messenger for the gods.*

Demeter had the care of all the plants, fruits, and grains in the world. She taught the people how to plough the fields and plant the seeds. She helped them gather their harvests. They loved the kind Earth Mother and gladly obeyed her. They also loved her daughter, the beautiful Persephone.

Persephone wandered all day in the meadows among the flowers. Wherever she went, birds, singing merrily, flocked after her. The people said, "Where Persephone is, there is the warm sunshine. Flowers bloom when she smiles. Listen to her voice: it is like a bird's song."

Hades asked Zeus to get him a bride to live with him in the Underworld. He had fallen in love with Persephone, but Zeus knew that Demeter would never agree to let her daughter marry Hades. Hades made a plan to carry off Persephone.

Demeter wished always to have her child near her. But, one day, Persephone went alone into a meadow near the sea. She made a wreath of delicate blossoms for her hair, and gathered all the flowers that her apron could hold. Far away across the meadow she saw a white flower gleaming. She ran to it and found it was a narcissus, but far more beautiful than any she had ever seen. On a single stem were a hundred blossoms. She tried to pick it, but the stem would not break. With all her strength she grasped it, and slowly the narcissus came up by the roots.

It left a great opening in the Earth. The mountain split open. Soon, Persephone heard a rumbling like thunder under her feet. Then she saw four black horses coming towards her from the opening. Behind them was a chariot made of gold and precious stones. In it sat a dark, stern man. It was Hades. He had come up from his land of darkness, and was shading his eyes with his hands. In the sunny meadow Hades saw Persephone standing, beautiful with flowers. He reached out and caught her in his arms, and placed her in the chariot beside him.

The flowers fell from her apron. "Oh, my lovely flowers!" she cried. "I have lost them all."

Then she saw the stern face of Hades. Frightened, she stretched out her hands to Helios, who was driving his sun horses across the sky and could not stop until day was done. She called to her mother, Demeter, for help. No one answered her.

Hades drove straight towards his dark underground home. The horses seemed to fly. As they left the light, Hades tried to comfort Persephone. He told her of the wonders of his kingdom, of all the gold and silver and precious stones which he possessed. In the dim light, as they went along, Persephone saw gems glittering on every side, but she did not care for them and she wept bitterly.

"I have been very lonely in my vast kingdom," said Hades. "I am bringing you to my palace, where you shall be my queen. You shall share all my riches with me."

But Persephone did not want to be a queen. She longed only for her mother and the bright sunshine and the sweet-smelling meadows.

Soon they came to the palace of Hades. It seemed very dark and dismal to Persephone, and very cold, too. A feast was ready for her, but she would not eat. She knew that anyone who ate in Hades' home could never again return to Earth. She was very unhappy, though Hades tried in many ways to please her.

Everything on the Earth was unhappy, too.

One by one the flowers hung their heads and said, "We cannot bloom, for Persephone has gone."

The trees dropped their leaves and moaned, "Persephone has gone, gone."

The birds flew away, calling, "We cannot sing, for Persephone has gone."

Demeter was more miserable than anyone else. She had heard Persephone call her, and had gone swiftly home to find her. She searched all the Earth for her child.

She asked everyone she met on her way these questions: "Have you seen Persephone? Where is Persephone?"

The only answer she ever received was, "Gone, gone. Persephone is gone!"

Soon, Demeter became a wrinkled old woman. No one would have known that she was the kind mother who had always smiled on the people. She sat mourning day and night, her great tears falling steadily upon the cold ground. Nothing grew upon the Earth and all became dreary and barren. It was useless for the people to plough the soil. It was useless to plant the seeds. Nothing could grow without the help of Demeter, and all the people were idle and sad.

Demeter wandered into many lands, and when she found no one on Earth who could tell her about Persephone, she looked up toward the sky. There she saw Helios in his bright chariot. He was not driving as high in the sky as he was wont to do. He had been hidden by dark mists so that no one had been able to see him for many days. Demeter knew that he must know about Persephone, for he could see all things on Earth and in the sky.

"Oh, great Helios," she cried, "pity me, and tell me where my child is hidden."

Then Helios told Demeter that Hades had carried Persephone away and that she was with him in his underground home.

Demeter hastened to great Father Zeus, who could do all things. She asked him to send to Hades for her daughter. Zeus called Hermes. He bade him to go as swiftly as the wind to the home of Hades.

Hermes gladly obeyed, and he whispered the joyful news to all that he met on his way. "I am going for Persephone. I am going for Persephone. Be ready to welcome her back!"

Hermes soon arrived in the gloomy kingdom under the Earth. He gave Hades the message from Zeus. He told about the barren Earth and of how Demeter was mourning for her child. He said she would not let anything grow until Persephone came back. "The people will starve if she does not soon return," he said.

Then Persephone wept bitterly, for that very day she had eaten a pomegranate and swallowed three of its seeds, and she remembered that whoever ate in Hades' home could never return to Earth again.

But Hades took pity upon her and said, "Go, Persephone, back to the sunshine. But the law must be obeyed, and you shall come back every year to stay with me one month for each seed that you have eaten. That is all I ask."

Joy gave her wings, and as swiftly as Hermes himself, Persephone flew up into the sunshine.

Suddenly, the flowers sprang up. The birds flocked together and sang; and the trees put on bright green leaves. Everything, great and small, began to say in its own language, "Be happy, for Persephone has come! Persephone has come!"

Demeter was so benumbed with sorrow that she did not at once heed these voices. But soon she saw the great changes all about her and was puzzled. "Can the Earth be ungrateful? Does it so soon forget my sweet Persephone?" she cried.

It was not long, however, before her own face grew radiant. She became once more the kind Earth Mother, for she held again her beloved child in her arms.

When Demeter found that Persephone could stay with her for only part of the year, she brought out the choicest treasures from the storehouse, and while Persephone stayed the world was filled with beauty and joy.

When she had gone, Demeter carefully covered the rivers and lakes and spread a soft white blanket over the sleeping Earth.

Exploring Myths

Ancient Greek Culture

There were two great poets in Ancient Greece—Homer and Hesiod. Their stories included the characters of Greek mythology, and were written about 700 BC. The Greeks believed that these men were great teachers. Their stories tell of the beginning of the world, and wars between the gods. They also tell of the Greek heroes who were almost as important to the Greeks as the gods. The stories about the mythical gods were the basis of the Greeks' religious life until CE 529.

The civilisation of Ancient Greece was more advanced than any before it. Ruins of some of the famous buildings that were built to honour the gods, such as the Parthenon, are still standing. Archaeologists still find fragments of wonderful artworks created by the Greeks, many of which feature the gods and goddesses.

The Parthenon

Explaining Events of the Natural World

Myths provided people in ancient times with explanations of natural events in the form of stories that could be easily understood. The myth of Persephone provided an explanation for the changes in seasons.

When Persephone was with Hades, the Earth became dark, cold and gloomy. Many plants lost their leaves and looked as if they were no longer alive, and the Earth was covered with a blanket of frost and snow. The Ancient Greeks believed this caused the winter season. When Persephone returned to the Earth, the sun brought warmth and plants began to grow and could be harvested. This explained the return of spring and summer.

Spring

Summer

Autumn

Winter

Mythical Beings

The characters in myths usually have magical powers. They use these powers to create natural features of the world.

The characters in the myth of Persephone are Greek gods and goddesses from the time of the Olympians. They were regarded as being immortal, divine beings. They had magical powers that enabled them to rule over the world. For example, Hades' power made the Earth open up as Persephone pulled up the narcissus, so he could come from the Underworld and take her to his kingdom.

Character Profiles

Demeter, Persephone's mother, was the most powerful of all the goddesses. She was the goddess of agriculture and ruled over all living things.

Zeus was the ruler of the gods and goddesses at Mount Olympus.

Hades was the ruler of the Underworld, and was a brother of Zeus.

Hermes was the son of Zeus. He was the messenger of the gods. He wore winged shoes to speed him on his way as he went about his work as messenger.

Helios was also a son of Zeus and was known as the god of the Sun.

Challenges for the Characters

The characters in myths often face tests or challenges. Persephone faced a challenge in the Underworld with Hades—to obey one rule. If she ate in Hades' home, she would never again return to Earth.

Character Relationships

A Character Relationship Chart is the simplest way to show the relationships between the main characters in a story. Examine the following Character Relationship Chart for *Persephone*.

HERMES
The messenger of the gods
Demeter is grateful to Hermes for returning her daughter to her.
Rescues Persephone from the Underworld.
PERSEPHONE
Daughter of Demeter
Hades is in love with Persephone and kidnaps her. He imprisons her in the Underworld.
HADES
Ruler of the Underworld

King Arthur
Robin Hood

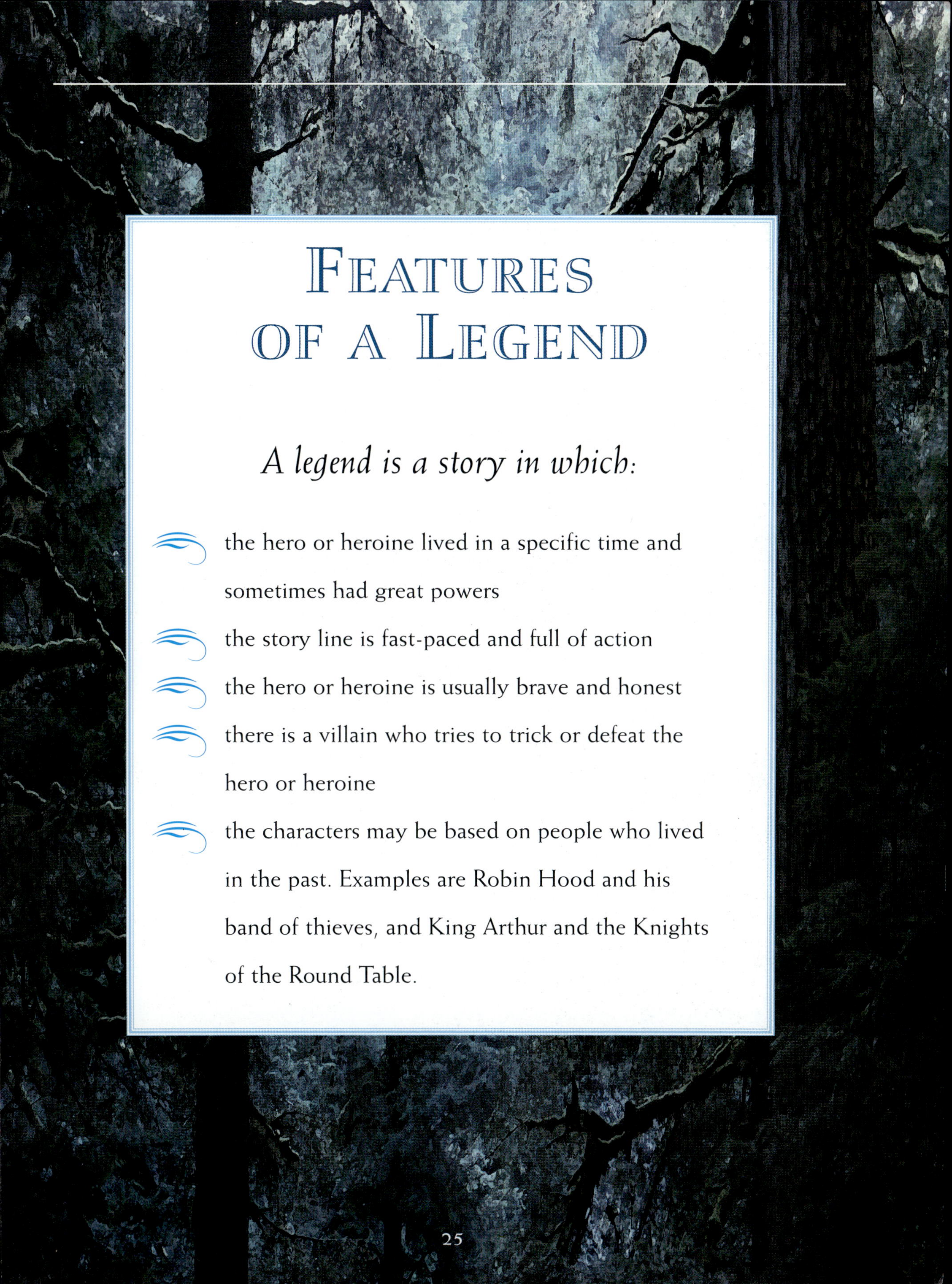

Features of a Legend

A legend is a story in which:

- the hero or heroine lived in a specific time and sometimes had great powers
- the story line is fast-paced and full of action
- the hero or heroine is usually brave and honest
- there is a villain who tries to trick or defeat the hero or heroine
- the characters may be based on people who lived in the past. Examples are Robin Hood and his band of thieves, and King Arthur and the Knights of the Round Table.

The Willow Pattern

The story of the Willow Pattern is a Chinese legend.

This story was told in China more than one thousand years ago. It became famous in Western countries after an English engraver, Thomas Minton, created the Willow Pattern that was printed on china plates in 1780. The pattern on the plates is said to represent the story.

Koong-se was the daughter of a rich, powerful man called T'so Ling. She was in love with Chang, a humble scribe who came every day to her father's house to write letters for him in his beautiful script. Chang was a poet, too, and he wrote poems to Koong-se, which she had to read in secret. There was no chance that they would ever marry; her father was too proud. Then Koong-se's maid had an idea. Why didn't the lovers meet in the little summer-house, which was tucked away in a corner of T'so Ling's enormous garden?

"Perfect," said Koong-se, when she saw it, and they started to meet there every day. Chang gave her his poems and she gave him some blue beads.

But old T'so Ling, who was always snooping about, found them there and flew into a great rage. Chang was sent away and told that he would be put to death if ever he returned. Koong-se's little maid was sent away, too.

Then T'so Ling had a huge fence built all round the house and a special terrace for his daughter to walk on, that jutted out into the garden. She could see the flowers, and the river with its great willow tree weeping into the water, but she couldn't reach them any more. And there was no chance of Chang's rowing up the river to snatch a glimpse of her either. T'so Ling's great hall, where he spent his day counting his money, had windows that looked down into the garden.

One day, T'so Ling told his daughter that she was to marry a great lord, a Ta-jin of enormous wealth. He too was old, and greedy. Koong-se wept. She knew she would be married to the hideous Ta-jin when the peach tree outside her window came into bloom. How she envied the birds their freedom as they flew in and out of its branches.

Chang, hearing about the marriage, wrote a poem and sent it down the river in a coconut shell. "If you become his wife," it said, "my poor heart will break."

"Then save me," begged Koong-se, sending back her message in the bobbing coconut shell.

But the days passed and no word came from Chang. The peach tree was nearly in blossom and in T'so Ling's house the marriage feast was being prepared. Koong-se was not to meet her husband till the wedding morning, but the night before, the two old men got very drunk and this was Chang's great chance. Stealing through the garden and into the house, he put on a coat belonging to one of T'so Ling's drunken servants, freed Koong-se from her chamber and crept away with her into the shadow of the willow tree. With her she brought her distaff, the special rod on which she wound her wool. From now on they would be poor and she would have to earn her living. Chang carried a box of jewels which the Ta-jin had brought as a wedding gift.

Something woke the sleeping T'so-Ling, and finding his daughter's room empty, he rushed out into the garden. There were the lovers, hurrying across the bridge. With terrible cries he pursued them but they were young, and he was a fat, drunk old man. By the time he reached the bridge they had disappeared, and although his servants hunted high and low for them, all trace of Koong-se and her beloved Chang had vanished.

For weeks T'so Ling's servants looked for them, but in vain. In fact, they were close at hand, living in a tiny gardener's cottage not very far from the house. They had been married there in secret, and they were very happy except that they could only venture outside after dark. By day the place swarmed with T'so Ling's servants and the Ta-jin had threatened to kill the young couple, if they ever showed their faces again. He was a proud man and he had been cheated of a beautiful wife, not to mention his jewels.

In the end Koong-se's father ordered soldiers to join the hunt for the vanished lovers. Someone had told him they might be hiding in the gardener's cottage. Up they marched to the door and banged so hard the little house shook. The gardener's wife, who was a clever woman, kept them talking and gave them food and drink while Chang and his bride made their escape. The river flowed behind the house, and although it was swollen with all the winter's rain, Chang plunged in and managed to swim to the opposite shore where a little boat was moored.

In this they made their escape, and when the soldiers at last forced their way into the cottage, they found only footprints on the floor, and an open window through which the cold night air was blowing.

After a long and dangerous journey on the great Yangtze Kiang River, Chang and Koong-se found a small deserted island where they set up house. Koong-se spun wool, Chang sold the Ta-jin's jewels to buy what they needed, and they lived there together in perfect contentment for many years. Chang planted seeds and his crops grew tall. He began to write poems again, and books about the simple country life, which had brought them such happiness.

But it was these very books that brought an end to everything for they became famous and the Ta-jin, that rich old man who had planned to marry Koong-se, read them and vowed even now to take his revenge. Gathering soldiers together he gave them cruel commands, and in no time at all they had found the secret island where Chang, the famous farmer and poet, lived.

Within minutes Chang lay dead, a sword through his heart, and poor Koong-se, unable to carry on living without her beloved Chang at her side, ran into the house and set fire to it.

But that isn't the end of the Willow Pattern Story, for the gods, moved to pity by the great love between Chang and Koong-se, turned them into two doves. And now they fly forever above the willow tree by the bridge, cooing softly to each other as the peach tree blossoms.

EXPLORING LEGENDS

In legends, the heroes and heroines lived in a specific time and place.

- Who are the hero and heroine of this story?
- In which country is the story set?
- How long ago might they have lived?

The heroes and heroines often have great powers.

- Although the hero and heroine did not have the power to stop their enemies, what happened after their death that demonstrated their great powers?

The characters may be based on people who once lived.

- In what way does this story sound as if it is based on a true event?

The hero and heroine of a legend are usually brave and honest.

- In what ways do the hero and heroine of *The Willow Pattern* show these strengths?
- One other character shows bravery, too. Who is this character? (see page 31.)

There is usually a villain, who tries to trick or defeat the hero and heroine.

- Which characters are the villains in the story?
- Why do you think each is a villain?

Legends are full of action. Climb up the story ladder of action in this story.

17 Two doves appeared in the sky.

16 Koong-se and Chang died.

15 The Ta-jin's soldiers found the island.

14 Koong-se and Chang lived on a deserted island.

13 The couple escaped in a boat on the Yangtze Kiang River.

12 T'so-Ling sent soldiers to the cottage.

11 They stayed at a gardener's cottage.

10 T'so-Ling saw the couple on the bridge.

9 T'so-Ling found Koong-se's room empty.

8 Chang came to rescue Koong-se.

7 Koong-se was about to marry the Ta-jin.

6 Koong-se asked Chang to rescue her.

5 T'so-Ling arranged for Koong-se to marry a rich old man.

4 T'so-Ling built a fence around the house to imprison Koong-se.

3 T'so-Ling discovered that Koong-se and Chang were in love.

2 Chang came to work for T'so-Ling.

1 Koong-se lived with her father, T'so-Ling.

Look at the design of the willow pattern plate.
Which parts of the story can you recognise?

You should be able to see the island, T'so-Ling's house, the fence he built to imprison Koong-se, the men on the bridge searching for the couple, the boat in which they made their escape, the fruit tree near the house and the doves above the bridge.

COMPREHENSION QUESTIONS

Persephone

Literal Comprehension

1 Why did Persephone go to the far side of the meadow?
2 How had Hades planned to take Persephone?
3 Why couldn't Helios help Persephone?
4 Why didn't Persephone join in the feast in the Underworld?
5 What happened on the Earth while Persephone was gone?
6 Who told Demeter where Persephone had gone?
7 Why wasn't Persephone completely happy about her release?

Inferential Comprehension

8 Why do you think the people loved Demeter?
9 Give three words that describe Persephone.
10 Why do you think Persephone wasn't impressed by Hades' gold, silver and gems?
11 Why do you think Hermes was pleased to be sent to rescue Persephone?
12 Why do you think Hades released Persephone?

Reflection

13 What natural events are explained in the story?
14 What lessons could Hades have learned?
15 What might Persephone have learned from her experience?

The Willow Pattern

Literal Comprehension

1 Why did Koong-se and Chang have to be secretive?

2 What steps did T'so-Ling take to keep his daughter away from others?

3 How did the couple plan to survive after their escape?

4 What was the last place that T'so-Ling saw his daughter?

5 Why was the Ta-jin so angry?

6 How did the couple escape?

7 How did Chang and Koong-se spend their time on the island?

8 How did the Ta-jin find out where the couple were living?

9 What happened to Chang?

10 What happened to Koong-se?

11 What did the gods do for the couple so that they could be together always?

Inferential Comprehension

12 Give four words that describe the Ta-jin.

13 How did Koong-se measure the passage of time?

Reflection

14 What lesson might the legend be telling to the people of that time?

Myths and Legends Genre Checklists

A MYTH is a story in which:

- events of the natural world are explained
- mythical beings, such as gods and goddesses, are often included
- the characters may face tests and challenges
- the values of a particular culture are reflected
- good usually triumphs over evil.

A LEGEND is a story in which:

- the hero and heroine lived in a specific time and sometimes had great powers
- the story line is fast-paced and full of action
- the main character is usually brave and honest
- there is a villain who tries to trick or defeat the hero or heroine
- the characters may be based on people who lived in the past. Examples are Robin Hood and his band of thieves or King Arthur and the Knights of the Round Table.